WITHDRAWN

Fun
Weather Days

by Pam Rosenberg

Children's Press®
A Division of Scholastic Inc.
New York Toronto London Auckland Sydney
Mexico City New Delhi Hong Kong
Danbury, Connecticut

These content vocabulary word builders are for grades 1–2.
Subject Consultants: Robert Van Winkle, Chief Meteorologist, WBBH, Fort Myers, Florida; and Jack Williams, Public Outreach Coordinator, American Meteorological Society, Boston, Massachusetts

Reading Consultant: Cecilia Minden-Cupp, PhD, Former Director, Language and Literacy Program, Harvard Graduate School of Education

Photographs © 2007: Corbis Images: 7 top right (Kevin Dodge), 20 top (Gavriel Jecan), 5 top left, 15 (Daniel Karmann/epa), 2, 5 bottom right, 10 (Pete Leonard/zefa), 21 bottom (Galen Rowell), 4 bottom left, 5 bottom left, 8, 17 (Royalty-Free), 7 bottom right, 23 top right, 23 bottom right (Ariel Skelley), 23 top left (Tom Stewart); Dembinsky Photo Assoc./Mark A. Schneider: 4 top, 13; Getty Images: cover (Wilhelm Scholz), 23 bottom left (Juan Silva/Photodisc Red); Kenneth G. Libbrecht/www.snowcrystals.com: 4 bottom right, 16; Masterfile: 7 top left (Boden/Ledingham), 9 (Lloyd Sutton); Photo Researchers, NY: 20 bottom (Pascal Goetgheluck), back cover, 5 top right, 11 (Larry Landolfi); Richard Carlson, www.pals.iastate.edu/carlson: 19; Superstock, Inc./Purestock: 1, 7 bottom left; Visuals Unlimited/John Sohlden: 21 top.

Book Design: Simonsays Design!
Book Production: The Design Lab

Library of Congress Cataloging-in-Publication Data
Rosenberg, Pam.
   Fun weather days / Pam Rosenberg.
      p. cm. — (Scholastic news nonfiction readers)
   Includes index.
   ISBN-10: 0-531-16772-0
   ISBN-13: 978-0-531-16772-4
   1. Weather—Juvenile literature. 2. Meteorology—Juvenile literature.
   I. Title. II. Series.
   QC981.5.T78 2007
   551.5—dc22   2006013304

1 2 3 4 5 6 7 8 9 10 R 16 15 14 13 12 11 10 09 08 07

CONTENTS

WORD HUNT

Look for these words as you read. They will be in **bold**.

clouds
(kloudz)

sky
(skye)

snow crystal
(snoh **kriss**-tuhl)

fog
(fawg)

rainbow
(**rayn**-boh)

snowflake
(**snoh**-flake)

sunlight
(**sun**-lite)

Fun in the Forecast

Any day can be a fun weather day. You just have to know what to look for. Let's go outside and see what is happening today!

Any time of year can
bring a fun weather day!

A springtime rain shower has just ended. The sun comes out behind you. A colorful arch appears in the **sky**. It is a **rainbow**!

sky

You can see many different colors in a rainbow. What colors do you see?

9

A rainbow is made of **sunlight** and water.

When sunlight shines through raindrops, the drops separate the sunlight's colors. This makes up the colors of a rainbow.

sunlight

Take a good look when you see a rainbow. It will soon disappear!

Lazy summer afternoons can be fun weather days, too. Let's watch some clouds roll by. Not all clouds look the same. Some are puffy and gray. Other clouds are thin and white.

Did you know that clouds are made of tiny drops of water? The drops fall from the cloud when they get big enough. Then it begins to rain.

There are always clouds in the sky somewhere in the world.

A chilly fall morning might bring **fog**. Fog is a cloud that is on or close to the ground.

Have you ever walked outside on a foggy day? The air feels damp. Things look kind of spooky!

Fog forms when the air near the ground is cool and wet.

You might see a **snow crystal** on a cold, cloudy winter day. Snow crystal is another name for a **snowflake**.

Big, fluffy snowflakes are made when a few snow crystals stick together.

snow crystal

No two snowflakes look exactly the same!

Every day can be a fun weather day. You may have snowflakes to catch, a rainbow to chase, or clouds to see. Keep watching the sky!

What does this cloud look like to you?

WHAT KINDS OF CLOUDS CAN YOU SEE IN THE SKY?

Cumulus clouds are puffy and white. Sometimes they look like fluffy pillows.

Cirrus clouds are thin and white. Sometimes they look like streamers.

Stratus clouds are gray. They often cover the sky like a blanket.

Cap clouds can be seen near mountains. They look like flying saucers!

YOUR NEW WORDS

clouds (kloudz) large groups of water drops in the air that are white or gray

fog (fawg) a cloud that is on or near the ground

rainbow (**rayn**-boh) a colorful arch formed when raindrops bend sunlight

sky (skye) the area that looks blue on a sunny day and seems to arch over Earth

snow crystal (snoh **kriss**-tuhl) water that freezes inside a cloud

snowflake (**snoh**-flake) a single snow crystal or a few snow crystals stuck together

sunlight (**sun**-lite) light from the sun

MORE WEATHER FUN

**Ice skating
on a cold
winter day**

**Kite flying
on a windy
spring day**

**Puddle jumping
on a rainy
summer day**

**Jumping in
leaves on a
cool fall day**

FIND OUT MORE
Book:
Bauer, Marion Dane. *Clouds.* New York, NY: Aladdin, 2004.

Website:
Web Weather for Kids
http://eo.ucar.edu/webweather

MEET THE AUTHOR:
Pam Rosenberg is an editor and author of children's books. She lives in Arlington Heights, Illinois. She likes to spend fun weather days with her kids, Sarah and Jake, and her husband, Peter.